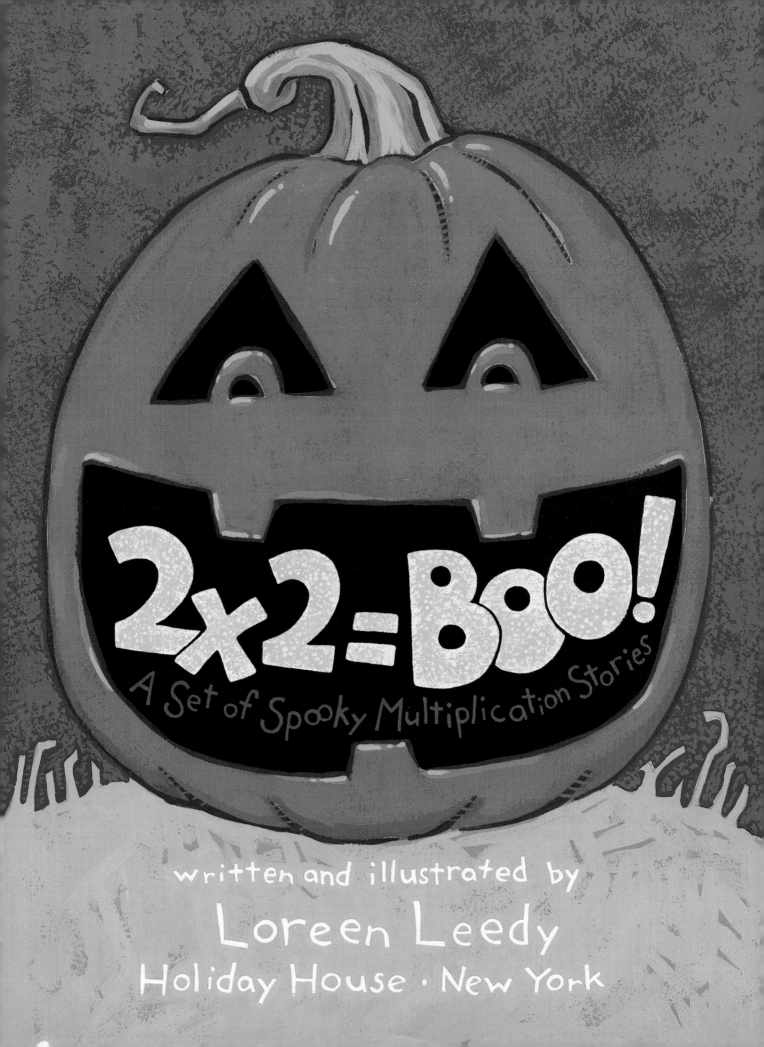

2x2=Boo!

A Set of Spooky Multiplication Stories

written and illustrated by

Loreen Leedy
Holiday House · New York

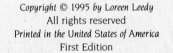

For Regina,
who likes the spider chandelier

Library of Congress Cataloging-in-Publication Data
Leedy, Loreen.
2 × 2 = boo! : a set of spooky multiplication stories / written
and illustrated by Loreen Leedy. — 1st ed.
        p.   cm.
ISBN 0-8234-1190-7
1. Multiplication—Juvenile literature.   [1. Multiplication.]
I. Title.
QA115.L443   1995   94-46711   CIP   AC
512.2'13—dc20

Contents

How do you make a vampire disappear?

How do you turn one bag of candy into five bags?

And how do you double a moose head?

All you have to do is MULTIPLY!

The first chapter is about multiplying with zero.

The next chapter is about multiplying with the number one.

Keep going, and by the time you've read all the stories, you will know the multiplication facts from 0 to 5.

Have fun!

The Disappearing Zero

I'll only be in the store for a few minutes.

Okay, Griselda.

Wait here, Inkling. I have some shopping to do.

See you later, Jinks.

Hi! My boss is buying frog toes.

How quaint.

She happens to be a very talented witch.

I'm sure.

Just the other day, a nasty vampire attacked us, so Griselda multiplied him by ZERO . . .
1x0=0!
. . . and made the vampire vanish!
I know—one vampire times ZERO equals ZERO vampires.

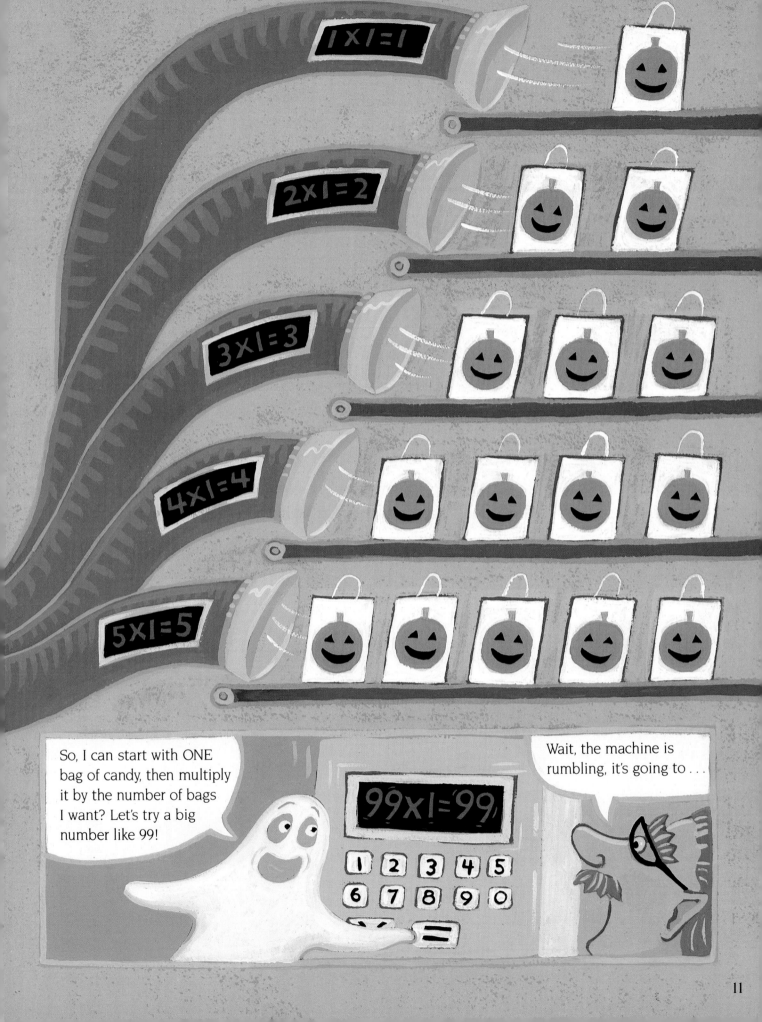

Seeing Double

I can't believe that Mom expects me to clean this entire attic.

Just look at all this old junk. Whose glasses are these?

Dr. Spook's Doublevision Spectacles

DIRECTIONS:
Put on glasses and stare at something. Multiply by two — the item will double.

23

CHAPTER 5

Boo Stew

Mr. Bones, we must get the stew ready for my dinner party tonight.

Yes, Mrs. Tibia.

This recipe is only for one serving, but there will be FIVE of us.

Don't worry, I can multiply each ingredient by FIVE.

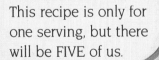

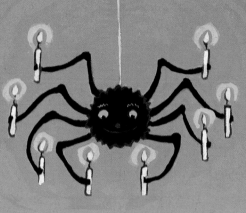

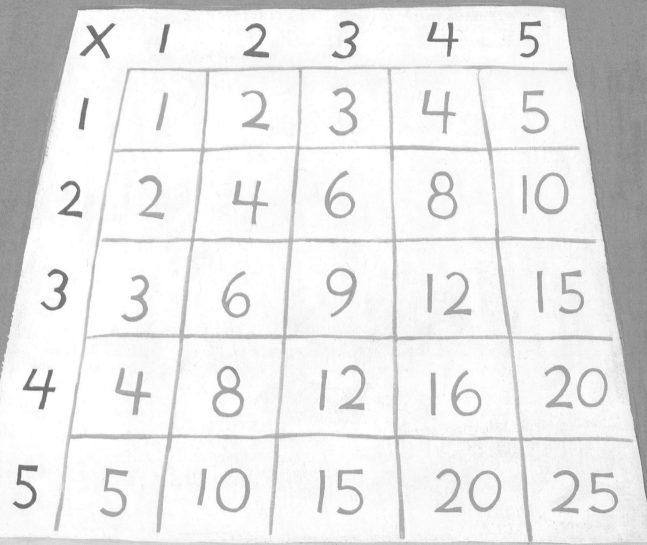

X	1	2	3	4	5
1	1	2	3	4	5
2	2	4	6	8	10
3	3	6	9	12	15
4	4	8	12	16	20
5	5	10	15	20	25

Now that's what I call a multiplication table!